FOREST HOUSE ™

This 1991 School and Library Edition published by FOREST HOUSE PUBLISHING COMPANY, INC.

Printed and bound in the United States of America.

Forest House Publishing Co., Inc.
P.O. Box 738
Lake Forest, Illinois 60045

ISBN 1-878363-28-X

Publisher's Cataloging in Publication Data

Hallinan, P.K.
   My very best rainy day/ written and illustrated by P.K. Hallinan. –

   p. cm. – (Books about awareness and caring)
   SUMMARY: All the wonderful things you can do – outdoors and in the
house, alone and with friends – on a rainy day.
   ISBN 1-878363-28-X

   1. [Stories in rhyme.]   2. [Rain.]   I. Title.   II. Series.

PZ8.3.H15   811.54
                          QBI90-244

It's a wonderful
nothing-to-do rainy day!
The rain's falling gently.
The world's a soft gray.

Just grab your umbrella
and be on your way.
It's a wonderful
nothing-to-do rainy day!

It's time to go splashing
on rain-covered lawns.

And time to go dashing
through puddles and ponds.

It's time for launching
a fabulous fleet
of walnut-shell sailboats
to sail past your feet.

7

When there's nothing to do
there's really no end
to the things you can think of,
or dream, or pretend.

You can work, if you like,
on fixing your bike.

You can mend the old dent
where your tow truck is bent.

You can even start building
a playhouse for two,
with a trapdoor so small
only you can crawl through.

You can bake a mud pie.

You can watch worms go by.

You can zoom all around
like a jet in the sky.

It's all up to you
what you do or you play
on this wonderful
nothing-to-do rainy day!

But maybe you'd rather
just stay warm and dry
and make up some games
that take you inside.

16

Like trying each crayon
on your coloring books . . .

or painting your face
just to see how it looks.

Or maybe it's time
to go up to your room
and set up a tent
with a bedspread and broom.

And then you can howl
like a great, hooting owl.

Then much later on,
about quarter to three,
there's nothing like popcorn
and a little TV.

Yes, you'll find that the grayest
of days can be bright
if you treat them like presents
from morning till night.

21

So don't ever worry
when the clouds start to form.
Just think of the wonders
that come with each storm . . .

22

A hot cup of cocoa,
a warm, cheery blaze . . .

and wonderful
nothing-to-do rainy days!